Colderon Fitzstanley is a retired banking and IT consultant who has developed a keen interest in his family history, part of which has been represented in this book. He had two careers during his working life, involving 30 years in international banking and a further 20 years in banking software, using his previous experience to enable international banks to be more effective.

Colderon Fitzstanley

WHY I'M NOT KING OF ENGLAND

Or Anywhere Else for that Matter

AUSTIN MACAULEY PUBLISHERS™

LONDON • CAMBRIDGE • NEW YORK • SHARJAH

A CIP catalogue record for this title is available from the British Library.

ISBN 9781528977401 (Paperback)
ISBN 9781528977425 (ePub e-book)

www.austinmacauley.com

First Published 2024
Austin Macauley Publishers Ltd®
1 Canada Square
Canary Wharf
London
E14 5AA

I have used Ancestry.co.uk, Geni.com and Wikipedia for some source material.

I blame Edward III, fair and square.

As I look back on my life, which has a rich history, and consider where I am today compared to where I might have been if I'd had the breaks, I have reached the conclusion that he is the cause of my problems.

Here I am, a good old South London lad, in my prime and despite having a loving family and having enjoyed a fruitful working life, which brought its various rewards, I'm left feeling unfulfilled because of Edward.

We had a similar start in life – getting introduced to the world in troubled times, and suffering trauma at a young age.

In my case, it was being evacuated from my spiritual homeland, Camberwell, to the wilds of Surrey late in 1944 whilst I was still a prisoner in my mother's womb. It was deemed necessary, apparently, and I was introduced to the world in Woking in January 1945. Having been safely delivered, my mother and I were shipped back to Camberwell after four days… Go figure.

It wasn't till later in life that I realised, despite my upbringing, this had deprived me of the right to call myself a true cockney – something my two younger brothers, who were born in Southwark, share in common and tease me about no end. On the plus side, there was a time during my career in the software industry, when I worked for a company based in

Woking. I was the only member of staff who was born in Woking, lived in Woking (courtesy of lodging with a friend who lived there to save myself a daily commute), and worked in Woking; although, the nature of the job meant it was only a base of operations.

Still, it made me unique, always something to be cherished.

Edward's trauma was different in some ways but took place at an earlier time and in different circumstances. I will tell you his story.

Edward 1ll

Edward was the son of Edward II, king of England, and Isabella of France, daughter to French King Philippe IV.

I suppose to put this into perspective and tie it up to my starting point for this memoir, I should point out that Edward II was one of my 20th great grandfathers whilst Isabella was one of my 19th great grandmothers in her own right. For the record and to keep the narrative in line with other books about my family history, the use of "my" in this context applies, as far as the history is concerned, to both my brothers as well as to me since we share the DNA, the trail of which brought this saga to light.

You will find that most of the characters I mention from here onwards are all ancestors of mine, no matter which side of the story they might seem to represent. The word ancestor in this context means that they were a great grandfather in a range of magnitude between 16 and 21. Not for nothing have I gathered all the stories under the general heading of "Family Feuds".

Edward II's story is worth a book to itself and, in fact, there is a memoir about him in the series "Family Feuds". Edward III, as a small boy, was used by his father to get himself out of a diplomatic difficulty of his own making.

Edward II (I will use their regnal numbers to maintain the differential) was required to pay homage to Charles IV, the French king, for the lands he held in France; however, as the king of England, he didn't want to do it. So, he passed ownership of the lands to his son, Edward III, and sent him instead to pay homage to the French King, accompanied by his mother.

In those days much importance was paid to the "pecking order", so to speak. Both England and France were operated by the feudal system where the monarch was the overlord for the country, and dukes and earls paid homage periodically, recognising that over-lordship belonged to the monarch. In this instance, the Duchies of Normandy and Aquitaine were held by the English crown with the French King being the feudal overlord, hence the homage.

Edward II, in an attempt to forestall domestic problems with his own barons by paying homage to a rival King, gave his son a problem that he would have to deal with in the future.

Meanwhile, the rebellious barons, whom Edward II was trying to placate, had their leader in exile in France. This man was Roger de Mortimer, the 1st earl of March, who was one of my ancestors. I have often thought that he may have been the source of the character Roger de Lodgerly played by Charles Hawtrey in "Carry on Henry." A bit out of sequence, but I don't think those films are meant to be taken literally. Edward's and Roger's stories accompanied by others are told in a companion book, as yet untitled.

Anyway, Isabella, who was by this time totally disenchanted with Edward and his bisexual behaviour, refused to return to England. She met Roger and they became allies in a common cause – getting rid of Edward II – and, inevitably, became lovers.

They raised an army with the support of Isabella's brother Charles and invaded England and overthrew Edward II replacing him with Edward III as a boy king, and with Roger and Isabella acting as Regents on Edward's behalf.

Edward III had to experience this without any powers until 1330 AD when he was able to raise an army of his own to capture and imprison Roger and Isabella, and take control of his own life and country. As I said, this story is told in some detail in a companion book, but the experiences left a scar on Edward.

He resolved to avoid the mistakes his father made; partly, because he was not subject to the same proclivities as his father, and he made a success of his life. He married Philippa of Hainault, who, coincidentally, was one of my ancestors in her own right, and they proceeded to have a happy and successful marriage.

I said "*made a success*" but, of course, he is the reason I'm writing this, so you may judge the relativity of his success.

As part of the general background, he reigned for fifty years, which was quite prodigious in mediaeval times and transformed England into one of the main military powers in Europe. He oversaw some vital developments in English legislation and government as well as the ravages of the Black Death. Well somebody had to and it might as well be him, as a kind of counterbalance to all the good things.

Edward married Philippa of Hainault in 1328 AD and they had a son Edward (later known as the Black Prince) two years later. This helped in providing Edward with the platform to topple Roger and Isabella. Once ensconced on the throne, he began the serious task of kinging. As a side issue, one of the problems with dynasties, particularly, the mediaeval ones, is the frequent recycling of names, which makes it very difficult for chroniclers to both track people and to differentiate them.

His father had been ineffective in fighting the Scots, so one of his early tasks was to take back control of the situation. Roger de Mortimer had, unfortunately, failed in the battle of Stanhope Park and the subsequent Treaty of Edinburgh had been very favourable to the Scots, leaving many English barons discontented.

These barons became known as "The Disinherited" and, like malcontents everywhere, began plotting. Edward conspired with them secretly and they invaded Scotland, winning the battle of Dupplin Moor. They also attempted to replace King David II of Scotland with Edward Balliol.

This succeeded up to a point and Edward, having besieged Berwick, was able to claim a victory and gain significant lands in Southern Scotland. In the grand scheme of things, this was a temporary victory and, gradually Balliol's reign was ended and David II was re-instated.

However, emboldened by this victory, Edward III declared himself the rightful heir to the throne of France, courtesy of his mother. In fact, he hoped to take advantage of one of those hiatuses that occurred frequently in the French royal family.

This action was brought about by the fact that Scotland and France had been in alliance for some time, which meant that England constantly had to be fighting on two fronts, often at the same time.

Aquitaine was, yet again, the focal point of the trouble. Philippe VI of France confiscated it instead of insisting on homage, as Edward had provided to his predecessor. So, Edward initiated his claim to the throne since he was Philippe IV's grandson whereas Philippe VI was his nephew. What larks the genealogists had in those days.

This was the start of what became known as "The Hundred Years", although, it actually went on a bit longer than that. It started well for England with victories at Crecy and Poitiers leading to the favourable Treaty of Brétigny, under which England made significant territorial gains in return for Edward giving up his claim to the throne. Nice to see the family business of extortion still thriving.

Shortly after the war started, he and Philippa had a second son, Lionel of Antwerp, who became the duke of Clarence. For the record, Lionel was one of my ancestors. This was followed by two more sons, John of Gaunt, who became duke of Lancaster, and Edmund of Langley, who became duke of York. Both of them were also my ancestors, and the seeds of the Wars of the Roses were sown.

Over the next 13 or so years they had 13 more children, some of whom died young, culminating in Thomas of Woodstock who became duke of Gloucester in 1355 AD. Thomas was also one of my ancestors, which gave me a very useful hand to play in genealogy… You'd think.

Meanwhile, Edward was still prosecuting the war against France by aligning himself with other powerful kings and princes in Europe, but the only tangible success from this strategy was to gain control of the English Channel.

There was discontent at home as the parliament started to complain about the cost of the war and Edward had to deal with it. Eventually, after a schism with the Archbishop of Canterbury, things were resolved and Edward was able to pursue his aims in France.

He took a great force over to Normandy and worked his way up the coast towards Flanders. He encountered a major French army at a village called Crecy, near the Somme, and despite being outnumbered, he defeated the French and put them to flight. He then spent a year laying siege to the town of Calais, which finally surrendered in 1347 AD.

Events in the following year caused a change of strategy. The Black Death struck England and caused a cessation of hostilities. Over a third of the population died and this put a strain on the entire economy since the plague hit farmworkers, other labourers and soldiers alike, causing major devastation in the countryside.

Fortunately for Edward, things recovered fairly quickly and by the mid-1350s, the situation in England was improving. Military action in France was re-commenced.

Edward, also called the Black Prince because of the colour of his armour, led a force of men to victory over a French army with superior numbers at the battle of Poitiers in 1356 AD. He captured the French King, who by then was John II, and his son Philip.

The French army was in disarray: their King was imprisoned and the central government had collapsed. Still, Edward couldn't achieve the final military success and hence, the treaty of Brétigny was signed in 1360 AD. In this treaty, Edward renounced his claim, however valid, to the French throne in return for keeping under English control his captured lands in Northern France along with Aquitaine and Gascony, which had been English for generations.

This freed him up to turn his attention to matters at home.

Parliament was established as a representative institution under his grandfather, Edward I, but it developed substantially during his reign. The English Baronage became more clearly defined and restricted to those who received personal summons to parliament. There were no free and fair elections in those days, unlike today.

This ran hand-in-hand with the evolution of parliament into a bi-cameral affair, with a House of Lords and a House of Commons and it was in the lower house where the greater changes took place. The procedure of impeachment of those who did wrong, and the office of Speaker, were created during Edward's reign.

During the war with France, it was perceived by the common people in England that the Papacy was largely controlled by the French government and papal taxation of the English Church and its parishioners was financing their enemies. So an act was passed, which aimed at reducing the papacy's ability to control the English courts and people and raise revenues from us. Thinking about it, that's not a million miles away from where we are today, vis a vis Brexit. What goes around, comes around.

No attempt was made to sever the ties between the Pope and the King since they needed each other, so the provisions were passed. Other important pieces of legislation were the Treason Act in 1351 AD and the reform of the Justices of the Peace.

They were given the power not only to investigate crimes and make arrests but to try cases, including those of felony or serious crime. These cases normally involved the theft of land and local courts were designed to deal with them.

The main political influence of the House of Commons lay in its hard-won right to grant taxes. The financial burdens of the foreign wars were enormous, and the King and his advisers tried many ways to cover the costs. There was always the income from the crown lands and the King was able to borrow from Italian and other financiers, which he did.

But to fight on the scale that Edward did, he needed to resort to the taxation of his subjects for which he needed parliament's approval. Taxation tended to take two forms – levy and customs.

The levy was based on a fixed percentage of the value of lands and buildings, which could produce a lot of money, but the King had to prove its necessity before it could be administered. Customs, on the other hand, were applied to the movements of specific products, such as wool, and could also provide a steady and reliable source of income, although they still needed to be approved by Parliament.

Through Edward's continual requirement for funding for his war effort, Parliament gained political influence throughout his reign through a system of quid pro quo. In order for a tax to be considered "just", the King had to prove its necessity and it had to be granted by the community of the realm (Parliament) for the benefit of that community. Additionally, Parliament would also present petitions for redress of grievances to the King, mostly concerned with misgovernment by the royal officials. This ensured the process was beneficial to both parties and formed the basis of rule by consent, which is the foundation of our modern-day constitutional monarchy.

Edward's policy throughout his reign was to rely on the upper reaches of the nobility for support in war and administration and, unlike his father and grandfather before him, he regularly created new earls who were beholden to him personally and on whom he could rely. He also created the title of duke for the close relatives, mostly his sons, as the senior level of the aristocracy.

He bolstered the sense of community within this group by creating the "Order of the Garter" as a chivalrous order of knights, based on the premise of the Arthurian legend.

Edward oversaw the establishment of English as the lingua franca, replacing French as the language of the court and of parliament and all new laws were published only in English from 1361 AD; although, it took some years before the process was completed.

From a family perspective, he became a grandfather several times in the period between 1367 AD and 1380 AD with the births of Richard II to the Black Prince, Henry Bolingbroke to John of Gaunt, Philippa of Clarence to Lionel, and Richard, Earl of Cambridge, to Edmund of York amongst others. Thus, his dynasty seemed secure.

Gradually his peers, with whom he'd grown up and trusted, died and their heirs had more in common with his own sons than himself. So, he began to loosen the reins a little. Increasingly, he began to rely on his sons to conduct military campaigns, which not always got notable success.

Lionel had attempted to subdue the semi-autonomous Irish Lords and the only tangible thing that came out of the venture was the repressive Statutes of Kilkenny. Meanwhile, John II of France had died in captivity whilst trying to raise his ransom and had been replaced as King by Charles V. Soon, Charles restarted hostilities and in 1369 AD John of Gaunt was given charge of an army to suppress him.

This failed and with the Treaty of Bordeaux six years later, England's French possessions were reduced to the towns of Calais, Bordeaux and Bayonne.

Meanwhile, on the domestic front, Edward had to cope with a fractious parliament which, since its foundation, had gradually wrested a lot of powers from the King. Its role was to oversee and permit the raising of revenue from taxes, which the King of the day used to wage war overseas. The lack of success of this activity was what led to the problems of parliament in 1376 AD.

The Black Death had given rise to a scarcity of labour, which caused wages to rise and, in an attempt to prevent this, the ruling class had instituted the Statute of Labourers, which sought to peg wages to their pre-plague levels and to remove the right of workers to move freely to seek employment elsewhere. Funny how some things never change, isn't it?

Gradually resentment built and it led to the Peasant's Revolt, which occurred four years after Edward's death. The so-called "good" parliament of 1376 AD was an attempt to address some of the grievances and this led to the dismissal of some of the King's closest advisors and his mistress because they had a great influence on state affairs. Then, permission was granted to raise further taxes. By now Edward was in ill health and, six months later, his eldest son, The Black Prince, died leaving his son Richard II as presumptive heir.

John of Gaunt immediately began to exert more influence and led royal opposition to parliament and its conduct, causing a recall of parliament the following year when most of its good work was undone. Edward died of a stroke within weeks of this and his ten-year-old grandson, Richard II became King.

Generally speaking, Edward III was not a statesman, although, he did possess qualities that might have made him a successful one. He was a warrior – ambitious, unscrupulous, selfish, extravagant (with other people's money), and ostentatious (viz. the Garter), and those attributes would make him a politician anywhere for any political party, in my opinion.

His obligations as a king sat very lightly with him, as they had done with some of his predecessors and, indeed, some successors. He felt bound by no special duty to either maintain the theory of royal supremacy or to follow a policy that would benefit his people. Like Richard 1 before him, he valued England as a source of supplies to pursue his personal goals.

So he was an admired and feared king who, due to bad luck (the premature death of his eldest son) coinciding with his own ill health, gave rise to the circumstances whereby I find myself writing this today.

Richard II

I, like many other people, cannot claim to be descended from Richard II since he had no children.

In some ways, he was lucky to survive since his father, grandfather and elder brother pre-deceased him in short order, leaving him as the young king of England, but I digress.

He was the second son of Edward, the Black Prince and Prince of Wales, who was the eldest son of Edward III. His mother was Joan of Kent who was, to say the least, an experienced married woman, even for those days, and one of my ancestors in her own right.

She was the granddaughter of Edward I, daughter of Edward II's half-brother who was her husband's grandfather. So, technically, she was his aunt and she had previously been married to Thomas Holland, 1st earl of Kent; also one of my ancestors. She was also married to William de Montacute, 2nd earl of Salisbury; although, that marriage was childless. The marriage between Edward and Joan required papal approval.

It's a good job, I'm not paranoid, else the amount of incest in my family history could keep me awake at night.

So, back to Richard's sorry story.

When his elder brother died, Richard was three. When he was nine his father died of dysentery, making him the apparent heir. Richard's grandfather died a year later, making him king, but requiring a regent.

The nobles were worried that if John of Gaunt, Richard's Uncle, was made regent, it would be devastating. So, following his father's death, Richard was hastily invested as the prince of Wales, making him heir apparent. Then, a council of ministers, excluding John of Gaunt, was appointed the following year to oversee the young King's passage to his majority.

Excluding Gaunt worked, but very little ran smoothly.

The war against France, which was still going on, was not going well for England. There were problems in the north with the Scots (nothing new there), and economic difficulties caused by the Black Death were still present and affecting economic growth. Basically, the peasantry wasn't happy.

To finance what was becoming an increasingly unpopular war, poll taxes were levied three times between 1377 AD and 1381 AD, the last one being the straw that broke the camel's back, to coin a phrase.

The roots of the conflict had lingered since the original Black Death and intermittent outbreaks of plague in the interim, and the unpopular Statute of Labourers, which were still being applied. Following the poll tax of 1381 AD, the rebellion started in Kent and Essex, the two wealthiest counties close to London.

It was led by Wat Tyler, John Ball and Jack Straw; they gathered at Blackheath and went on to burn down John of Gaunt's Savoy Palace. The Lord Chancellor and the Treasurer were both killed by the mob, who were demanding the complete abolition of serfdom.

The young King was sheltering with his councillors in the Tower of London and it was agreed that the Crown did not have the forces to combat the rebels; so, they decided to negotiate.

The two sides met at Mile End and agreed to the rebel's demands, which emboldened them, and they went on a killing and looting spree. They met again the following day at Smithfield and Richard reiterated his promises, but Wat Tyler was not convinced about his sincerity. An altercation broke out and William Walworth, the mayor of London, pulled Tyler from his horse and killed him with his sword. This stunned the crowd and whilst they considered their next move, Richard moved to their head, saying: "*I am your Captain, follow me*", and led the mob away from the scene.

Meanwhile, Walworth, who was one of my ancestors, perhaps unsurprisingly, gathered together a force to combat the rebels. However, Richard granted clemency and allowed the rebels to disperse and return to their homes.

However, as a true leader, he conveniently forgot his promises, and revoked the charters of freedom and pardon that he had issued. Next, he went to Essex to suppress any rebellion, ending it at a skirmish at Billericay, which he won convincingly.

This effectively marked the time when he came of age and ruled in his own name, as he had shown great courage and determination by handling the rebellion. Unfortunately for him, the episode impressed upon his young mind, the dangers of disobedience and threats to royal authority helped shape his absolutist approach to kinging, which was the trademark of his reign.

He married Anne of Bohemia, daughter of the Holy Roman Emperor, which was of diplomatic importance, bringing another ally to the ongoing war against France. Sadly, it didn't achieve any success and the marriage was childless. Anne died from the plague in 1394 AD and was mourned by Richard.

During this period, Edmund de Mortimer, one of my ancestors, had married Philippa of Clarence, Lionel's daughter, and became one of the leading supporters of Richard in parliament, leading the opposition to John of Gaunt and serving on the council that steered Richard to manhood, so to speak.

He was Earl Marshal of England and died fighting in Ireland on the King's behalf. His son, Roger, was considered as next in line to the throne, the heir presumptive. Roger was a great-grandson of Edward III and married to Richard's half-niece (a complicated family), he spent most of his life in Ireland and stayed out of political intrigue in England. He was one of my ancestors and was within touching distance of being a king.

It was Richard's lack of children, with no hope of having any, which was at the heart of concern. John of Gaunt, supported by his youngest brother Thomas, was the senior uncle of the King since Lionel had died some 10 years before the Black Prince. John of Gaunt had his own agenda and was the de facto leader of the lords who were opposed to Richard's use of favourites (a common enough problem for English kings as it seems) to influence his thinking.

In 1387 AD, things came to a head when the Lords Appellant, as they became known, took over the central government and dismissed the King's favourites.

Once again it was the long-running war in France that was at the heart of it. Richard's two uncles urged a large-scale, inevitably expensive, campaign to protect English possessions, and hopefully gain more. Whereas, Richard favoured a smaller incursion led by Henry le Despenser, Bishop of Norwich, which failed miserably. In those days many priests were warriors, so it paid to attend mass every week.

Richard then turned on Scotland, leading a small army northward to no effect since they didn't engage with the enemy. Relations between Richard and his uncle deteriorated, and John of Gaunt left England to pursue his claim to the throne of Castile… There was always something.

In John's absence, the leadership of the dissenting group fell to Thomas, duke of Gloucester, and Richard Fitzalan, earl of Arundel; both of whom were ancestors of mine.

With the threat of an invasion by France growing, Chancellor Michael de la Pole, yet another ancestor of mine, requested more money from parliament in the form of yet another tax. Rather than consenting, parliament refused to consider any request until the Chancellor was removed and, reluctantly, Richard agreed.

Richard was affronted by the actions of parliament and embarked on a tour of the country in an attempt to muster support for his cause and installed his favourite Robert de Vere, earl of Oxford, as justice of Chester to prepare a military power base in Cheshire. He also obtained a ruling from the Chief Justice that parliament's conduct had been unlawful and treasonable.

When he returned to London, his uncle Thomas; Fitzalan; Thomas de Beauchamp, earl of Warwick, and a distant cousin of mine brought charges of treason against Richard's major supporters, including de la Pole and de Vere. Say what you like, my family gets everywhere.

Richard stalled negotiations to gain time since he was expecting de Vere to arrive at any time with his army. The three Earls, however, along with Henry Bolingbroke (John of Gaunt's son) and Thomas de Mowbray, earl of Nottingham, another ancestor, intercepted de Vere at Radcot Bridge and routed him. This forced de Vere to flee the country.

Richard now had no choice but to accept the appellants' demands, and they proceeded to break up the circle of favourites that had surrounded the King.

He gradually re-established royal authority, aided somewhat by the return of John of Gaunt who reconciled with Richard and lent him his support, allowing Richard to rule peacefully for the next eight years.

Internally, though, he was in turmoil and allowed the events to fester until 1397 AD when he took revenge on the appellants. He had the Earls of Gloucester (his uncle), Arundel and Warwick arrested for their parts in the events eight years earlier since he then felt secure enough to act against them.

Arundel was the first to be tried, found guilty and executed; his brother, who was Archbishop of Canterbury, was forced into exile. Gloucester was being held in Calais, awaiting trial, when news arrived that he had died in captivity. Suspicion still exists that he had been killed on Richard's orders because he couldn't bring himself to have his uncle, a blood relation, publicly executed.

Warwick was also tried and found guilty, but his life was spared and he was sentenced to life imprisonment. Given the state of mediaeval prisons and the treatment of prisoners, I'm not sure it did him any favours.

Richard then took his vengeance on a tour of the regions, focusing on the localities of the Lords Appellant. He recruited retainers for his own purposes whilst prosecuting local men who had been loyal to the appellants. The fines levied on these men brought a vast amount of income to the treasury, but there were questions about the legality of the proceedings. In true, absolutist, kingly style, Richard just ignored the niceties and went about his business.

It is likely that he could not have behaved in this manner without the support or collusion of John of Gaunt, but he did have support from a growing number of opponents of John of Gaunt, many of whom were rewarded with new titles.

These included Henry Bolingbroke (who had switched sides and was then earl of Derby) who was made duke of Hereford, and Thomas de Mowbray (who had also switched sides) and was made duke of Norfolk. Also, Richard's half-brothers, John and Thomas Holland, were promoted to dukes of Exeter and Surrey respectively. Both of them were ancestors of mine.

Further recipients of Richard's magnanimity were John of Gaunt's son, John Beaufort; John Montacute, earl of Salisbury; and Lord Thomas le Despenser, earl of Gloucester. They are all cousins whose stories intermingle, unsurprisingly.

However, Richard's paranoia convinced him that there was still a threat to his authority in the form of the House of Lancaster, notwithstanding his favourable treatment of Beaufort. His fears were over John of Gaunt and his eldest son Henry Bolingbroke. They represented the wealthiest family in

England and were of royal descent and, as such, likely candidates to succeed the childless Richard.

In December 1397 AD, an argument started between Mowbray and Bolingbroke, the two former Lords Appellant. Bolingbroke claimed Mowbray had suggested they were next in line for royal retribution, which Mowbray vehemently denied since it was a treasonous suggestion and would have cried out for retribution. A parliamentary committee decided the two should resolve their differences by battle, but Richard decided on exile instead – Mowbray for life, Bolingbroke for ten years.

Six months later, he convened a parliament at Shrewsbury at which it was declared that all the acts of the previous parliament, which shackled Richard, were null and void, and that no restraint could legally be put on the King. Instead, its powers were transferred to a committee of twelve Lords and six Commoners, chosen from Richard's friends, making him an absolute ruler with no need to call parliament again.

A few months later, John of Gaunt died and rather than allowing Bolingbroke to succeed him as duke of Lancaster, Richard extended the term of his exile to life and expropriated his properties. Jealousy and fear, when allied together, make terrible advisers... Just saying.

He felt safe from Bolingbroke, who was residing in Paris since the French had little interest in challenging Richard and his peace policy, which was working well for both sides. He then left the country for another expedition to Ireland.

Unfortunately for him, Louis, the duke of Orleans, had gained control of the French court on the grounds of the insanity of Charles Vl of France. The policy of rapprochement with the English did not suit Louis' political ambitions, so he allowed Bolingbroke to leave for England with a small group of followers.

Henry and his men landed in Yorkshire and as the news spread, men from all over the country soon rallied around him, seeing him as hope for relief from Richard's oppression. He met with Henry Percy, earl of Northumberland, and other ancestors of mine who had misgivings about Richard's rule. Henry assured Percy that his only objective was to regain his lands and titles. Taking him at his word, Percy declined to interfere and his son, Harry "Hotspur", joined Henry's supporters.

Richard had taken most of his household knights and the loyal members of nobility with him to Ireland, so Henry met little resistance as he worked his way south. His Uncle Edmund, duke of York, who was acting as the keeper of the realm in Richard's absence, had little choice but to side with him since resistance was futile, to borrow a phrase from Richard Adams.

Richard eventually returned to England and made his way to Conwy, where he met with Percy for negotiations. A week later he surrendered to Bolingbroke at Flint Castle, promising to abdicate if his life was spared. Both men and their troops then returned to London with an indignant Richard who was forced to ride behind Henry all the way. On arrival, Richard was imprisoned in the Tower of London.

By now, Henry had changed his mind and was determined to take the throne of England, notwithstanding the rights of anybody else. Presenting the rationale for this was problematic.

There was no doubt that Richard's tyranny and misgovernment made him unworthy of being the king, but

Henry was not next in line for the throne. That distinction lay with Roger de Mortimer, as I have already mentioned, who was descended from Henry's father's elder brother, Lionel of Antwerp.

Henry's side claimed that de Mortimer's claim came through a female line whereas Henry was a direct male descendant, albeit junior, which gave him precedence in a male-dominated society.

Richard appeared before parliament and affirmed his willingness to give up his crown and accept his deposition because of his own unworthiness as a monarch. Nobody will ever know what it took for him to perform those acts, but a month later Henry Bolingbroke, duke of Lancaster, was crowned as King Henry IV of England.

The rest of Richard's life is unclear. He was held in the Tower and then Pontefract Castle, and Henry IV may have been willing to let him live but for the Epiphany Rising plot.

It was discovered that some demoted nobles, loyal followers of Richard – including the former Earls of Huntingdon, Kent and Salisbury – were plotting to overthrow Henry and reinstate Richard the following January.

Although the plot was foiled, it highlighted to Henry the danger that Richard posed so, unsurprisingly, he died soon afterward. Whether he starved himself to death, the official version, or met his end another way, it is not clear. What's clear is, he died and his actions in life had caused a major shift in the future rule of England.

He was buried in King's Langley Priory in 1400 AD, but in later years his body was moved to Westminster Abbey, where it lies today.

So, there you have it. Richard wasn't a good king by any means and brought about his own premature end through his actions. He probably would never have had children so the succession crisis would have occurred eventually, perhaps, with the same result... we will never know. That's the way life seems to work, never knowing how the alternative may have worked out.

I'll continue with the story as it unfolded.

Edward's Other Children

Lionel of Antwerp, Duke of Clarence

Lionel was the second oldest son of Edward III and one of my ancestors, as previously mentioned. He was actually born in Antwerp, the home of his mother Philippa of Hainault. When I look at my entire ancestry, I'm a bit of a mongrel I'm afraid.

He grew up to be a fine figure of a man, nearly seven feet tall with an athletic build. Sadly, for all concerned, he didn't live long in the big scheme of things.

He was betrothed as a child to Elizabeth de Burgh, daughter of William who was the 3rd earl of Ulster, and they were married in 1352 AD, but before that, he had gained possession of her great Irish inheritance when her father died and he became earl of Ulster in 1347 AD.

He expended a considerable amount of energy on the affairs of Ireland and was appointed governor in 1361 AD. The following year he was created duke of Clarence by his father after making an abortive attempt to secure the Scottish crown on his behalf. These Normans were nothing if not acquisitive.

His efforts to gain effective control of Ireland were only moderately successful and, having passed the Statutes of Kilkenny five years later, he dropped the task and returned to

England. The reason for the Statutes was that since the Norman reign began, English nobles had settled in Ireland and adapted to Irish life. They spoke Gaelic, followed Irish customs, married Irish women, and generally became more Irish than the indigenous population. The Statutes sought to bring an end to this by banning such practices in the future and forcing both communities to live separately – an early form of apartheid if you wish.

Naturally, the Statutes were unpopular, and things pretty much continued unchanged.

When he returned to England, the poet Geoffrey Chaucer became a page in his household but became much more later.

He and Elizabeth had a daughter, Philippa, who was born in 1355 AD in Ireland. Elizabeth died when Philippa was eight and Lionel felt that she needed a mother to help her into adulthood. So, he married the daughter of the Lord of Pavia in Italy and journeyed to Italy to collect his wife and dowry.

They married in Milan in 1368 AD and spent some months enjoying festivities during which Lionel got ill and died in Alba. It was suspected but never proven that he had been poisoned by his father-in-law. Where's the royal taster when you need him, eh?

Now an orphan, Philippa was married to Edmund de Mortimer, the 3rd earl of March, the following year. They began to have children, starting with a daughter, Anne, the following year.

It took several daughters and five years before a son and heir, Roger de Mortimer, was born to be endowed with her inheritance and titles. After the death of his father, Roger was the 4th earl of March and the 6th earl of Ulster, and one of my 17th great grandfathers.

On the death of his mother in 1382 AD, he became the presumptive heir to the crown since Richard II had no children. His sister Elizabeth, who was two years older than him, married Harry "Hotspur" Percy, who became a fervent supporter of Henry Bolingbroke in his struggles against Richard II.

Roger himself married Alianore, daughter of Thomas Holland who was Richard's half-brother. Their daughter, Anne Mortimer, married into the Yorkist branch of the Royal family and was the mother of Richard Plantagenet, the 3rd duke of York, Edward lV's father."

In the fullness of time, the House of York would base its claim to the throne of England on this linear connection and Lionel was the ancestor of the Yorkist kings and all subsequent British rulers beginning with Henry VIII since Henry VII married Elizabeth of York, Edward IV's daughter.

This is what leaves his mark in history.

John of Gaunt, Duke of Lancaster

John of Gaunt was the third son of Edward and one of my ancestors; I am descended from two of his daughters.

He grew up in the royal court, receiving every benefit that his position could bring him. He grew up to be a nobleman, soldier and statesman. He took his name from the place of his birth, Ghent, then known as Gand. Later, this easily adapted in the English tongue to Gaunt.

He married several times, becoming richer and acquiring more land through each marriage. His first wife was Blanche of Lancaster who was the granddaughter of Edmund

Crouchback, Edward I's brother, and hence his cousin. She was also one of my ancestors in her own right.

The marriage was part of Edward III's attempts to arrange advantageous marriages for each of his children and on the death of his father-in-law in 1361 AD, John became earl of Lancaster and received half his lands, making him the greatest landowner in the north of England. He inherited the rest of the lands when his sister-in-law died without children.

He was made duke of Lancaster by his father the following year. By then, he owned at least thirty castles and estates in England and France and had a household comparable in scale to that of a monarch. He had land in most of the counties in England and received a net income of between eight and ten thousand pounds a year. He was a powerful and wealthy man.

He and Blanche had several children, but most of them died young. The notable ones were Filippa, who married the King of Portugal, Henry Bolingbroke, whom I have already mentioned, and Elizabeth, one of his daughters from whom I am descended.

When Blanche died in 1368 AD, he married again, this time to Constance of Castile with whom he had a daughter, Catalina, who married the King of Castile.

Being of royal blood he also had a mistress, Katherine Swynford, with whom he had several illegitimate children, although they were "legitimised" when he married Katherine following Constance's death. All his children by Katherine carried the name of Beaufort, after a former French possession of John's but, significantly, they were later excluded from inheriting the throne by the questionable actions of their half-brother Henry. This was, presumably, an act of self-defence in his aim of retaining the usurped crown. Of these children, the notable ones were John, Thomas and Joan, of whom more later.

As Edward III got older, John of Gaunt along with his brothers got more involved with governing the country, particularly, with regard to foreign wars, such as the prolonged war against the French.

Sadly for John, he was not particularly successful in the war and, following the loss of territory, bore the brunt of the people's opposition to the conflict, particularly the mounting costs.

So he became more unpopular at home, mostly because his father and older brother Edward (Lionel had died by this time) were ailing and he wasn't. However, he retained great influence in parliament, serving on behalf of his father and promoting his interests. Following the deaths within a year of his elder brother and the King, John's position was deemed threatening.

The other nobles feared to have a boy king, Richard II, John's nephew, being influenced by John and having John as regent. So they invested Richard first as Prince of Wales and then as the King, aided by a council of ministers, specifically excluding John.

Notwithstanding that, John remained influential in parliament but made sure that his name was never associated with any action that might be construed as opposing the King, even though that is what he did. It was the taxes that he sought to introduce that led to the Peasant's Revolt and the burning of his Savoy Palace, even though he wasn't at home at the time.

John responded by going off to Castile to pursue a claim to the throne there that he had assumed from his wife Constance. He returned a year later, having failed in his mission, to find a crisis enveloping the country. He persuaded the Lords Appellant and his nephew to compromise and bring about a period of relative peace.

During this time, there was peace, however uneasy, and John's reputation was mostly restored.

However, due to Richard's growing paranoia and his need to avenge the affronts to his rule as king, John's position came under threat, particularly after his son and heir, Henry Bolingbroke, was exiled to France in 1398. John died the following year and Richard confiscated his titles and estates rather than have Henry inherit them. Also, he increased the severity of Henry's exile, thus, making his position untenable. We know about the consequences.

As Duke of Lancaster, John is seen as the founder of the House of Lancaster, which provided kings of England until the Wars of the Roses, when the right to wear the crown was disputed by the House of York, descended from his younger brother Edmund.

Through his children, he is an ancestor to all Scottish Monarchs beginning in 1437 AD and of all English Monarchs belonging to the houses of York and Tudor. This makes him an ancestor of all subsequent rulers of England.

Through his eldest daughter, all Portuguese Monarchs starting in 1433 AD descend from him, and through another daughter, he has among his descendants all monarchs of Castile from 1406 AD, and subsequently all those of a united Spain. Finally, he is also an ancestor of the Habsburgs who reigned in Spain and Austria, and other parts of Europe.

He was also a patron and friend of Geoffrey Chaucer and, near the end of their lives, they became brothers-in-law. John's third wife, Katherine, was the sister of Chaucer's wife, and John and Katherine's children, the Beauforts, were Chaucer's nephews and niece.

John of Gaunt's Children

Henry Bolingbroke

Henry was the eldest son of John of Gaunt but, as far as I can trace, we are not descended from him; the best relationship would be a distant cousin.

His story, leading up to usurp the crown, has already been partly told. He was born at Bolingbroke Castle, hence his name, and lived within the court of Richard II until the later years of his reign when Richard began to perceive him as a threat.

When his father married for the third time, legitimising Henry's half-siblings, things began to change. His legitimate sisters posed him no threat, but he was concerned about his three half-brothers.

His relationship with Katherine, his stepmother, was positive. Ralph Neville, who was also one of my ancestors and Henry's brother-in-law (he was married to Joan Beaufort), was one of his strongest supporters as was his eldest half-brother, John Beaufort. Thomas Swynford, a stepbrother, being a child of Katherine's first marriage, was another loyal companion and was constable of Pontefract Castle, where Richard II conveniently died.

To enrich the mix, Joan and Ralph had a daughter, Cecily, who married Richard, duke of York, of whom, more later.

Henry IV because of the manner in which he had obtained the crown, spent most of his reign combating plots, rebellions and assassination attempts, many of them instigated by one man.

The first rebellion occurred within months of Henry taking the throne and was planned to take place at the Epiphany in January, hence its name. John Montagu; earl of Salisbury, John Holland; earl of Huntingdon, Thomas Holland; his brother and earl of Kent, and Thomas le Despenser along with others planned to kidnap Henry during a tournament, kill him, and replace him with Richard.

Once discovered, the plot failed and the plotters fled, but they were all captured and summarily executed by beheading. Although he survived, Henry was thereafter on alert and it became obvious to him that Richard, even in captivity, was a threat that needed to be removed. 'Nuff said.

Between 1400 AD and 1415 AD, the Glendower uprising in Wales took place, which was led by Owen Glendower, the last Welshman to hold the title Prince of Wales. His story is told in detail in a companion book, "Why I'm not Prince of Wales."

There were three rebellions led by the Percy family at this time. The Battle of Shrewsbury took place in 1403 AD when Harry "Hotspur" Percy, who was one of my ancestors and had been a supporter of Henry, joined forces with Owen Glendower but was killed in the battle. His father, the earl of Northumberland fled.

Then, two years later the Earl was back, attempting a rebellion in Northern England which also failed. The other plotters were killed, but Northumberland fled to safety in Scotland. He was back three years later but was killed at the

Battle of Bramham Moor, and for the rest of Henry's reign, things were relatively peaceful.

Henry had married Mary de Bohun in 1380 AD, and she was one of our ancestors in her own right. They had several children, the most notable being Henry of Monmouth, later Henry V.

It was this Henry who led the army against the rebellions and who showed great military ability. As Henry IV's health gradually declined, his son took over more and more power, ending as an effective regent by 1410 AD. Henry died three years later.

Henry V's story is told in detail in a companion explanation about the Wars of the Roses, but for the purposes of this memoir, he ruled effectively until 1422 AD, supported by members of the de Mortimer family. This was despite their having been deprived of the crown by the actions of his father; Henry married Catherine de Valois, daughter of Charles Vl, king of France, and had a son who would be Henry Vl.

It was Henry Vl who became embroiled in the War of the Roses with the rival House of York, which led to years of fighting and, ultimately, the end of the Plantagenet rule of England, since kings and princes on both sides died in the fighting and eventually there was no direct male heir left on either side.

It fell to the genealogists to discover a Welshman, Henry Tudor, as the leading contender. He was a half-grandson of Henry Vl since Catherine de Valois had remarried Owen Tudor whose son married Margaret Beaufort, great-grand-daughter of John of Gaunt. How ironic that the successor to the Lancastrians, who had gained the throne by belittling the legitimate claims of a female ancestor of their rivals, came to rely on the same kind of relationship to further their own claims.

The waters now become very muddy, but it's safe to say that from here on my family tree had been firmly pushed on to a branch line, to mix metaphors.

I shall revert to Henry Tudor later but, as a further irony, his 6th great grandfather was Ednyfed Fychan, seneschal for Llewleyn Fawr of Wales. Ednyfed had two sons, the other one being my ancestor.

Joan Beaufort

Joan Beaufort was the half-sister of Henry IV and the only daughter of John of Gaunt and Katherine Swynford. As such, she was one of my ancestors in her own right.

John arranged for her to marry Robert Ferrers and they had two daughters before Robert died in 1395 AD. We are not descended from either of the daughters.

She then married Ralph Neville, 1st earl of Westmorland, who was, coincidentally, one of my ancestors, and recently widowed. He already had twelve children but wasn't satisfied with that, so he and Joan had fourteen of their own. He died in 1425 AD, probably of exhaustion, leaving Joan a wealthy widow and one of the greatest landowners in the north of England.

Ralph had been a supporter of Henry IV, and he and Joan used their position to arrange favourable marriages for their many offspring. One of the key marriages, for the purposes of my story is Eleanor who married Sir Henry Percy, the son of Harry Hotspur, and one of my ancestors. It's amazing how many of these noble families liked to recycle names – this

Henry Percy was the eighth one, as far as I can tell, and there were plenty more to follow. I can assure you that it makes the job of a chronicler very difficult at times.

Nobles often purchased the wardships of children orphaned by aristocratic rebellions, another useful form of revenue for the King who always needed money for something or other. In 1423 AD, they purchased the wardship of Richard of York and Henry's cousin came to live with them at Raby Castle. Eventually, Richard married their daughter, Cecily.

With so many children to marry off, this period of time witnessed the most amazing series of child marriages in English history and, by the time of her death, Joan was the mother of an earl, three barons, a countess, three duchesses, a bishop and a nun, just for good measure.

After Ralph died, his title passed to the eldest son of his first marriage, but much of his property was transferred to Joan's eldest son, Richard Neville, 5th earl of Salisbury, which sparked off the Neville-Neville feud that lasted throughout the Wars of the Roses.

John Beaufort

John was the eldest son of John of Gaunt and his third wife. He and his siblings were illegitimate at birth, but John legitimised them by marrying their mother when his second wife died and getting papal acceptance of their status. Despite this, Henry IV, their half-brother, barred their path to accession to the throne which, given later events seems to have been overlooked, if not ignored.

He was created earl of Somerset in 1397 AD, soon after his legitimacy was recognised, and was also made constable of Dover Castle and warden of the Cinque Ports. He was of assistance to Richard II in getting rid of the Lords Appellant, including his half-brother, for which he was rewarded with further honours, being made marquess of Somerset and marquess of Dorset, and being included in the Order of the Garter. For a good measure, he married Margaret Holland, sister of Thomas Holland who has been previously mentioned.

He remained in favour with Richard, even though Henry was exiled. When Henry replaced Richard, he rescinded John's elevations to a marquess, and John reverted to being earl of Somerset, but nonetheless remained loyal to Henry.

He and Margaret had several children; the notable ones being John, who became 1st duke of Somerset, and Joan. Joan married James 1 of Scotland, who has been mentioned previously. John had a daughter Margaret, mother of Henry Tudor, who has also been mentioned previously. Since she was a Beaufort and proscribed by Henry IV from being in the succession, there must have been dirty work at the crossroads for Henry Tudor to become king… That's all I'm saying.

Elizabeth Plantagenet

Elizabeth was John of Gaunt's daughter from his first wife, Blanche of Lancaster, and was one of my ancestors. She was brought up by Katherine Swynford, whom she held in great regard.

She was married at the age of seventeen to John Hastings, earl of Pembroke, who was only eight at the time, and moved to another household more befitting her rank as the countess; although, the marriage was annulled six years later.

At the age of twenty-three, she was tired of her adolescent husband and, it is rumoured, had been seduced by John Holland and was pregnant with his child. Gaunt arranged the annulment followed by a hasty marriage to Holland, 1st duke of Exeter.

Together, Elizabeth and John had six children of whom the important one, for the purposes of my story, is Constance who married Sir John Grey, another one of my ancestors.

John Holland was executed in 1400 AD for his part in the Epiphany Rising against his cousin and brother-in-law, and Elizabeth married Sir John Cornwall later that year. However, he had failed to seek permission from Henry to marry his sister and was imprisoned. Eventually, he was released, and they went on to have two children, neither of which figures in this story.

Edmund of Langley, Duke of York

Edmund was the fourth son of Edward III and Philippa of Hainault and took his name from his birthplace, Kings Langley in Hertfordshire. He was one of my ancestors.

He was made duke of York at the same time his brothers received their honours, but it was his younger son's marriage to a de Mortimer heiress that sparked the House of York to eventually make a claim for the throne.

On the death of his godfather, the Earl of Surrey, he was granted the Earl's lands to the north of the Trent, primarily in Yorkshire. He accompanied his father on an unsuccessful expedition in France, following which he was made a knight of the Garter. The following year he was created earl of Cambridge by his father.

During the 1370s he campaigned a lot in France. He supported his elder brother, the Black Prince, John Hastings and Edmund de Mortimer, earl of March. He also aided another elder brother, John of Gaunt, militarily in his claim to the crown of Castile.

He married Isabella of Castile, who was the sister of John of Gaunt's second wife (nothing like keeping it in the family), and they had three children: Edward, Constance and Richard, of whom more later.

Edmund acted as keeper of the Realm whilst his nephew, Richard II, was campaigning in Ireland in the mid-1390s and again in 1399 AD, when another nephew, Henry Bolingbroke, landed at Bridlington on his return from exile.

He had been left with scant military resources to resist Henry so he decided to join him instead, for which he was rewarded later.

It transpired from Richard II's will that Edmund was highly emphasised as his heir, despite the stronger claims of Roger de Mortimer and Henry. Seemingly, because Richard wanted to see Edmund's son, Edward, on the throne eventually.

Edmund died in 1402 AD at his birthplace and was buried there. From his children, his elder son Edward inherited his title and died at the Battle of Agincourt. He had no children.

Constance of York, his daughter, married Thomas le Despenser and then had an affair with Edmund Holland, son of Thomas, by whom she had an illegitimate daughter Eleanor. She married James Touchet, who was one of my ancestors.

His second son was Richard of Conisburgh, who became the 3rd earl of Cambridge. He married Anne de Mortimer, daughter of Roger de Mortimer, and they had several children, one of whom was Richard, the 3rd duke of York. Conisburgh was beheaded for his part in the Southampton Plot, which was designed to replace Henry V with Edmund de Mortimer.

Richard, the 3rd duke of York, was the father of Edward IV and Richard III, both Yorkist kings of England during the Wars of the Roses. Also, he was the grandfather of Elizabeth of York, who married Henry Tudor, from whom all subsequent monarchs of England are descended.

Through his mother, he inherited the Mortimer claim to the crown which, allied to his own lineage, put him in a very powerful position in the country, and his inherited lands made him very wealthy. It is no wonder that Henry V thought long and hard before allowing him to succeed in his lands and titles. He was merely storing up trouble for his own son, a trait that ran in the family.

In his later life, Henry VI became incapacitated and could not govern the country. So, Richard, as the premier earl, was appointed Protector of the Realm, the closest he got to be King. This lasted two years, after which Henry recovered and resumed his role as king.

Hostilities, later known as the Wars of the Roses, began in 1459 AD and Richard died the following year, with his second son, Edward, pursuing his claim to the throne and becoming king twice during the war.

When the war was finally finished, after the Battle of Bosworth, the damage caused to both halves of the Plantagenets was irrecoverable. Male descendants died in the battles or were killed whilst minors. So, in this last battle, the

Lancastrian troops were led by Henry Tudor who following his victory became known as Henry VII and married Elizabeth, daughter of Edward IV, in an attempt to reunite the country.

It is said that Henry VII was cursed and that he and his sons failed to produce heirs to their throne, and events tend to bear this out in part. Henry's first son died young and his second son was Henry VIII, and we know what happened then. The Tudors survived for one hundred years but only through their daughters, who had no heirs of their own.

The replacements, the Stuarts – descendants of one of Henry VII's daughters – failed to produce heirs. Eventually, they had to use James 1's daughter, who had married a Hanoverian prince, to provide the line that leads to the current monarch. Giving precedence to women in the line of descent came too late for me, I'm afraid.

That's a simple view and additional factors, such as the establishment of the Church of England by Henry VIII and the subsequent disqualifications of Catholics from the line of succession, played their part in the process.

However, my ancestors were in the mix, so to speak, until the advent of Henry VII. Since then, we have been on a branch line and not on the main line, but I have one card left to play.

Thomas of Woodstock, Duke of Gloucester

Thomas was the youngest son of Edward III and another one of my ancestors. He was born in Woodstock, Oxfordshire, and married Eleanor de Bohun, who was also one of my ancestors in her own right; her sister Mary married Henry Bolingbroke, Thomas' nephew.

He was given Pleshey Castle in Essex and made constable of the Realm. To keep pace with his relatives, he was knighted, made earl of Buckingham and was created duke of Gloucester at the same time as his brothers received their dukedoms.

He had a mixed military career, serving both his father Edward III and his nephew, Richard II, without distinction, but emerged alive. He was the leader of the Lords Appellant, who opposed Richard and after the rebellion collapsed, he was captured and held in prison in Calais, awaiting trial.

He died there in 1397 AD, probably, because Richard could not risk executing a blood relative in public but could live with rumours about how his uncle died, supposedly, at the hands of Thomas de Mowbray, who was also an ancestor of mine.

He left a widow and five children but, because of his treachery, his titles were forfeit. His eldest son Humphrey died just two years after him with no heirs; his youngest daughter died young; one entered a nunnery, and his second daughter died in childbirth.

Fortunately for me and this memoir, his eldest daughter Anne of Gloucester married three times. The third time to William Bourchier, who was also one of my ancestors.

William Bourchier, Comte l'Eu

William Bourchier was a descendant of a noble family in Essex who was a feudal tenant of Thomas Woodstock, and later he became Count of Eu, an old Norman title.

He entered Thomas' service as a young man and fought alongside him in several campaigns. When Thomas was arrested, and subsequently died, he was required by Richard to take command of the troops and pay an annual levy because of his association with Thomas.

Things changed under Henry IV and William was brought into the royal household to serve Henry of Monmouth, the future Henry V. This was when William was knighted and soon after this, he was assisting Anne of Gloucester, who had recently been widowed for the second time, in preparing the defences of Huntington Castle on the Welsh borders. They fell in love and were soon married.

Anne was one of the wealthiest women in England, which worked to William's advantage over time. William continued to be a loyal servant of Henry V and went to France on his behalf to negotiate a peace treaty with France even though, as it transpired, Henry had no intention of making peace.

When Henry invaded France the following year, William accompanied him and fought alongside him at Agincourt, earning a distinction. In the aftermath, he was made constable of the Tower of London, replacing the Duke of York who had died there. Later he was made Comte d'Eu, one of six places that Henry captured in his successful campaign.

He died in France in a battle at Troyes, leaving his wife to complete the upbringing of their children and arrange suitable marriages for them, which she did.

The eldest son Henry became the 1st earl of Essex and was married to Isabel of Cambridge, sister of the Duke of York; we are not descended from him.

The second son, named William after his father, married Thomasina Hankford, the heiress of the Fitzwarin family, and became the 9th baron Fitzwarin. He was one of my ancestors.

William Bourchier, 9ᵗʰ Baron Fitzwarin

William did not lead an outstanding life but was summoned to Parliament as Lord Fitzwarin, the title which he had inherited from his wife Thomasina.

He became more noted for his descendants, courtesy of his children and their marriages – Fulk Bourchier, 10ᵗʰ Baron, who was his son and heir, and Blanche, his daughter, from whom we are descended.

As a side-note, Fulk's son was John Bourchier, who was created first earl of Bath.

Blanche Bourchier

Blanche was the daughter of William Bourchier and Thomasina Hankford, and one of my 15ᵗʰ great-grandmothers in her own right.

She married Philip Beaumont, but they had no children and he died in 1473 AD. She then married Bartholomew St Leger, who was a son of the Sheriff of Kent.

They had a daughter, Anne, who married Alexander Woods, a commoner.

Bartholomew's eldest brother Sir Thomas had a granddaughter who married the 2ⁿᵈ earl of Bath; their descendants, the Fairfax's, would start out as supporters of Charles 1 and then become prominent generals in the parliamentary army under Oliver Cromwell. His elder brother Sir James married the daughter of Thomas Butler and was an uncle to Thomas Boleyn, earl of Wiltshire, father of Anne.

This marked the end of my direct links with the upper echelon of English society, and details of those ancestors that follow are hard to find and are certainly not of note, except to my own family. Having said that, several members of the Carpenter family, who were descended from French nobles, served as MP for various constituencies in the West of England.

So there you have it. My connections to royalty are via the female side of the various generations at a time when those connections were not assigned the equal validity they have today. Furthermore, double standards seem to have been applied by the people who sanctioned Henry IV's claim to the throne (by conquest) and later Henry Tudor (also by conquest) but also by virtue of his descent from a granddaughter of Edward III.

Am I bitter? Not really. The problems of primogeniture and illegitimacy also play their part in the selection process, but it's nice to have the connection; although, I know I'm not alone in this.

Printed in Great Britain
by Amazon